Poems and

Flowers

Poems and *Flowers*

Etta Wolpert

NODIN PRESS

ISBN: 978-1-932472-76-9

Library of Congress Control Number: 2008929453

Nodin Press, LCC
530 North Third Street
Suite 120
Minneapolis, MN 55401

Table of Contents

Beyond Youth

Life can be affirmed
Beyond youth.
Love is possible
At every age.
There is the thrill
Of the beauty of art,
Music, literature,
Companionship.
There is the fulfillment
Of age—times lived through;
Making some sense of things.

Excellence

They didn't say, "Kindness";
They said, "Excellence."
Yet maybe excellence
Is the greatest kindness;
And kindness is the
Greatest excellence.

"Visi d'Arte"

I couldn't say,
"Visi d'Arte";
Rather:
"Keep one heart
From breaking."
But maybe
That is what
Art does.

Snow

Somehow the thought
Of snow
Falling on my grave
Moves me.
I tried so hard.

Choice

It I had a choice
Of being born or not
I think I would choose
To be born.
I think I welcome
Being a brief part
Of the human enterprise,
To do my small part
To make life better.

Like Stained Glass

Past experiences are like
Stained glass windows.
They can be illuminated
And one can see them fully
Only when the light
Of one's present moment
Shines through them.

Affirm

Instead of only hoping,
I have come to affirm
A principle of good
At work in human society.
Not to acknowledge it
Would be ingratitude.

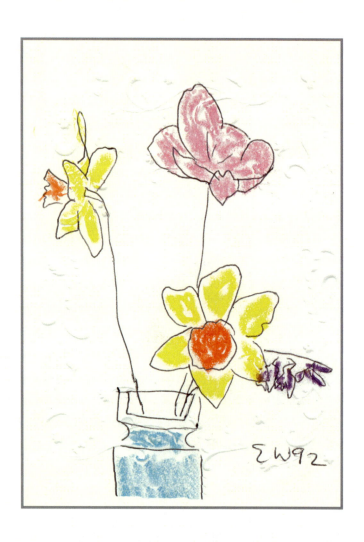

A Violin Concerto

Mendelssohn's *Violin Concerto*
Captures the
Essence of life
Better than any other
Work of art I know—
All its bittersweetness.

Angst

Picasso gives
Visual form
to twentieth-century
Existentialism—
His tortured faces
And his battle
of Guernica.

Sunshine

Liquid sunshine—
I bathe in it.
I drink it down.
The flowers, too,
Share in it.

Nugget

Each day contains
A nugget of gold
That we must sift out
With our sieves,
Or we may miss it.

A Continuum

There are two kinds
Of happiness:
Selfish happiness
And unselfish.
Or maybe it's
A continuum,
On a scale from
One to ten.

Both

Whether the glass
Is half-full or
Half-empty is
Up to you because
Either is true.
It is just what
Makes you feel better.

And then of course
Isn't it also the case
That both,
At the same time,
Are true?

MIT Grad Student

I suddenly had a
Vision of a woman
Being a gradute
Student at MIT
Who could make a lot
Of money from patents
On her inventions.
Her life would be
Interesting and free
Of dependence on a man
For money—
Interesting and
Challenging in that
She was using her brain.

People

My relationship to people
Is more important to me
Than whether there is
A benevolent Creator.
Love and kindness and
The adventure of life
Is enough for me.

Haiku

Anticipation instead of
Anxiety—that's what
I long to feel.

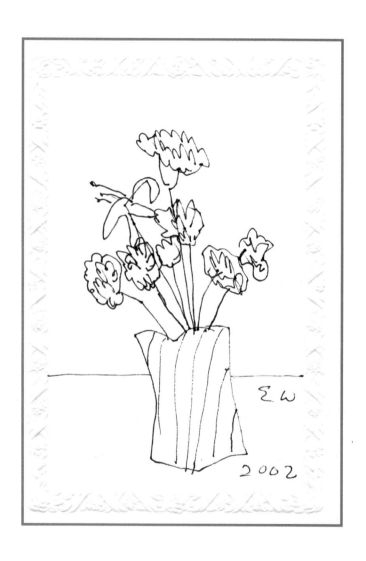

My Brother

You and I ran and ran
Thru the pasture
And the swamp
Amid weeds
Taller than we were,
When you were four
And I was five.

Weaving

I took threads of love
From many people
And wove them together
To form the fabric
Of my life.

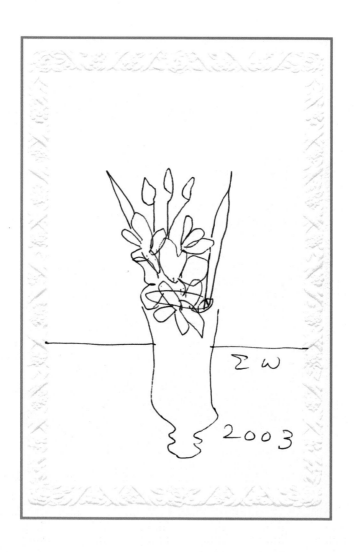

Health

Most of the time
The body works
Beautifully. It's an
Amazing construct.
I am gratified
That most living
Things are full of
Health, which is mostly
Unnoticed.

Nature

I must write about
The beauty—
Capture it in images
That sing.
In the Spring
There are apple blossoms.
In Summer, the ocean.
In Fall, the shattering maples.
In Winter, dusk.

Ew

2003

Reminded

We lose sight
Of the beauty,
Goodness and truth
All around us.
We need to be
Reminded.
I welcome reminding.

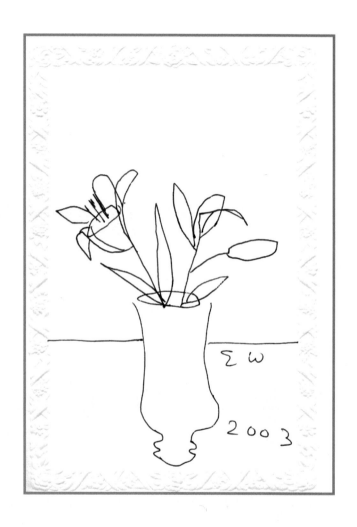

Plan Something

You say
It is depressing
To help unhappy
People but I see
Happy warriors
Doing it.
One must plan
A happy life
For oneself
To go with
Amelioration.

Ew

2003

Upbeat

It pays off
To be upbeat
Because things
Are apt to become
What you think
They are.

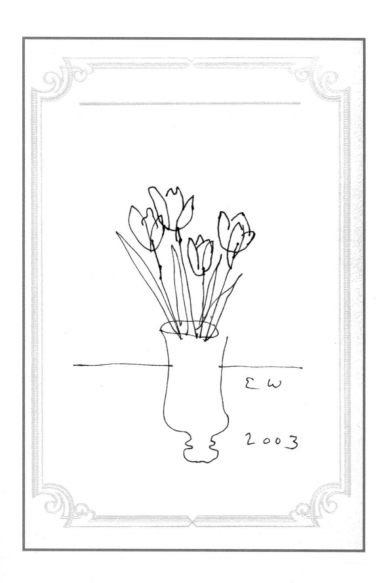

Literature

Greek tragedy shows
The beauty and rightness
Of goodness.
All great literature
Does that;
Makes us feel it—
To give our
Heartfelt assent.

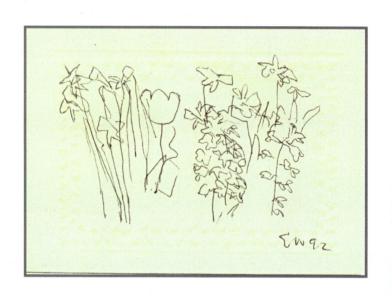

Filtering

Filtering down
Into the afternoon,
The success of work
On a painting that
Morning.

About the Author

Etta Wolpert was born in Minneapolis, Minnesota, in 1930. She studied art in her youth at the Minneapolis School of Art, and later attended the University of Minnesota where she earned a B.A. and M.A. in English and worked as the poet Allen Tate's graduate assistant. She also studied English at Columbia University graduate school with Lionel Trilling and Jacques Barzun.

Wolpert also studied at the Morris Davidson School of Modern Art in Provincetown, MA. She moved to Cambridge, MA, where she was a supervisor at the Harvard Bureau of Study Council. She has also taught at Emerson College in Boston, at the Cambridge Center for Adult Education, Brandeis, and at Northern Essex Community College. She has lived most of her life in Lexington, MA.